That Which Can Be Heard

Shruti Chauhan

Burning Eye

BurningEyeBooks
Never Knowingly
Mainstream

This edition published by Burning Eye Books 2018

www.burningeye.co.uk

@burningeyebooks

Burning Eye Books
15 West Hill, Portishead, BS20 6LG

ISBN 978-1-911570-49-3

For those I heard first

Shruti

[ʃruʈi]; Sanskrit: श्रुति

noun
That which can be heard.

Contents

Worlds

again and again   people ask me
about the words that make up
my language   and I always
say   *they are not words*
they are worlds

       the Gujarati word for country carries
       a world within   and when my grandfather
       places his wrinkled hand atop my head   tells
       me he is returning to his *desh* for the winter
       a world unfurls

a world of love and longing
of piggybacks across the ocean
of TB-stricken loneliness   pay packets
and passports   a world in
search of a better world

       at the temple I hear
       Om   shantih   shantih   shantih
       tucked into this plea for peace
       there are tides   energy
       galaxies   and eternity
       shantih   peace for I
          shantih   peace for us
             shantih   peace for the universe

recalling my sister's wedding day
I tear up at *vidai*
what's that? I'm asked   and I
refuse to reduce the word to
'the final stage of a Hindu wedding
ceremony when the bride bids
farewell to her family'

how do I say   all the
words of the English language
are redundant in the face of this
word   and no word can
contain the pain of this moment?

when the bride sobs into her
father's chest   she sees the
times he hushed a weeping
wound   sees the nights they
chased the moon together

and when she scatters rice over her
head   she hears her mother calling
up the stairs   hears the
stories that lulled
her to sleep

how do I say *vidai* bears
the contents of the life a bride
leaves behind   a world
forsaken in time?

again and again   people ask me
about the words that make up
my language   and I always
say   *they are not words*
they are worlds

Buttons

I wish life came with buttons:
fast-forward, rewind, play, stop, pause –
I want them all. I wish life came with buttons.
To meddle and meet with memories,
I wish life came with buttons.

Press play.
That winter morning when the brace that
had bullied my teeth for years retreated.
I grinned white and straight and full.
Rewind, play, rewind, play that day again.

Play.
Year 8. Three best friends drawing on
strawberry red Chupa Chups,
skipping arm in arm out of fifth period science.
Then two tear themselves from one.
Hey, we're not really your friends, they say.
We've just been using you because you're smart.
I swallow. Mum said betrayal tastes like red chilli –
nothing, then a sudden kick – but no,
betrayal tastes like strawberry red Chupa Chups.
I swallow again.
Press forward. Fast-forward.

Play.
Friday afternoons meant papier-mâché.
Gallons and tubs of PVA glue freckled our
five-year-old selves. We ruled a kingdom of PVA:
PVA milk crates, PVA boards, PVA book-corners,
PVA floor. But later's what we really waited for,
later when the glue had set: that wondrous
feeling of peeling dried glue from our hands.
Pause. Frame that feeling.

Play.
Developing breasts came at a price when,
age thirteen, the sound of a car door slamming
changed forever.
YH01 MHL, I told the pot-bellied policeman
sitting in my living room.
Are you sure?
Yes.
He scribbled it down. *And then what happened?*
The black car tailed me on the way home.
One of them got out, followed me, cornered me,
greasily telling me that he adored me,
that since he saw me, he knew that he loved me,
knew that he—
Stop.

Play.
2005 and the withered outline of a girl
hunched over a toilet bowl, knuckles stinging,
stomach singing, the smell of acid in the air.
Two fingers stuffed down her throat,
searching for that flap of skin.
For this? Not stop or forward; hit record
and tape over it with an episode of Friends.
I wish life came with buttons.

Caught in the Wind

There are things that stick:
the morning quiet accosted by high-strung horns,
the chill seeping into Ahmedabad's December,
blankets wrenched out from hidden pockets
in the high walls of our house,
socks and sweaters swirled into laundry,
rotla crumbled into khaki-coloured soup,
stray dogs tucking themselves deeper
into street corners, and Gauri,
the woman who did the dishes.

Knee-joints long jammed, she'd roll in
on her haunches like a choppy tide.
Cracked-earth hands and weighted breath.
Her husband a red rage most days, and
her sunburnt skin keeping the purples and
greens of his blows a secret.

Her son barring her one night from the house
she'd built. Her setting up camp in the front yard,
daughter-in-law tossing her scraps,
four-year-old grandson growing to regard her
a tumour and refusing her tender calls for her *dikro*.

Gauri hungry. Gauri grazing like a cow for love.
Gauri's failing bones.

But Gauri never wept.
Instead, she'd ease into the wash-pit,
bunch sari into lap and sing:
Lata, Asha, Rafi – the songs she'd
caught in the wind between
houses were hers.

Indian Whispers

Hey, did you notice? Her hair's thinning, it's only a matter of time before she's pinning it into a whisper of a bun – d'you remember, she'd sit sneering at balding guys she'd never date, how the tables have— Turn on your timestamp, please? See if he's been online. Oh, he has? What? Why hasn't he replied? What's with the mind games? That's it – I've had— It makes me sick that a man his age visits sites like those, even though he's married with kids and his kids have kids – d'you think they know? I'm like whoa, what's the world coming to? Are you coming too? I need you to. I know I'm going to need a shoulder or two once I see her on his arm. Forever, he said, we'd be one and the same, one pulse, one breath, till she strutted in, all manicured and middle-parted – d'you think they're really happy? Yeah, that's true, she's at her mum's an awful lot, at least twice a week. Well, hate to say it, but if he'd picked me… No. Way. She's been promoted this soon? She joined months after you. I bet it's something to do with her fulsome rack, or late nights at work giving the boss a hand. Didn't someone rap on his door once, to no response, but heard a muted thud, a muffled rustling, a pause and then… actually I'd better not— Say that again – another holiday? It's their third this year! I didn't realise he was doing so well. Didn't he fail his A-levels or something? He'd spend all his frees in the canteen playing Cheat, stacking card pyramids, vexing dinner ladies, playing tag with suspension. Now he's globe-hopping while we're not, we who wouldn't skive, turned in work on time, never a foot out of line; how is this— She said *what* about me? How dare she? When I've dropped her at the station on Sundays, whipped up blueberry cheesecake for her birthdays, given her alibis, let her use my Russian Red lipstick. I just can't believe it! Sick! It makes me sick that people have nothing better to do than talk about others.

Relations

The first time I heard the words 'uncle' and 'aunt',
my face crumpled itself into a question mark.
Miss Pegg scoured the words onto the board,
and on the floor, I shifted.

My hand shot up – she chose to ignore it.
Miss? I implored, and instead of a 'Yes?'
she brought a stern finger to her lip.

I groaned.

She didn't let me ask, what type of an
uncle? What type of an aunt? Were they
from my mother's side or my father's?

'Uncle', for me, was crammed with obscurity,
and 'aunt', well, it felt incomplete,
because I knew the truth!

An aunt wasn't an aunt, she was a *kaki*,
a *masi*, a *fui* or a *mami*, and an uncle wasn't
an uncle, he was a *masa*, a *fua*, a *kaka* or an *ada*.

*Miss Pegg, I cried, this aunt-uncle business
is utter confusion – confusion that is so easy to fix:
a Gujarati suffix is all that is needed.*

*Add kaka to the back of a name,
he's your father's little brother, add masi to a name,
she's the sister of your mother, and mami, easy,
she's your mother's brother's wife, and your father's
sister's husband is simply fua! Like Usha Kaki,
Raj Mama, Jayshree Masi, Amit Ada.*

*Can't you see, Miss Pegg, it doesn't have
to be complicated! You just need to tidy this
aunt-uncle mess!*

The Secret

Roll it in your palms and flatten it softly,
she advised. My heels were heavier than hers,
the balls flatter.

In dough she saw dinner,
while my hands dreamed a platter
of arm-in-arm flour dolls,

and only I, the Queen Planter,
knew what would happen
if they were planted:

in seconds they'd surge from the soil,
tresses suddenly plaited, and they'd
skip down the side of the—

Shruti! I said flatten lightly.

This Voice

named itself in Sanskrit

Shruti that which can be heard

ever ready to tread the path of symphony

this voice never slept

squalling for a sound in the silence

for a song in the darkness

this voice skipped words   slipped straight into

Sa Re Ga Ma Pa   into *Raga Shivranjani*

this voice sipped sonnets   similes   soliloquies

high   sometimes low

this voice simmered

                    now silky   stormy

this voice

                        somersaults

sings stories

                        that which can be heard

this voice

                    never

                                sleeps

Mehndi Night

They said Indian patterns would be best:
the peacocks, the paisleys, of course the girl-boy faces,
and they said his name should be a whisper
in your hand and that the rose-petalled sheets
would wait until he traced it, and they said
you should seal it with lemon and sugar,
and even if it itched and the smell of wet made you sick,
you should sleep with it on, and they said, the next day,
you shouldn't wash as water weakens the stain,
and they said, instead, you heat your hands over a stove,
and the darker the coppered hue,
the deeper his love.

And you on that red stool in the middle of the room,
you said,

Okay.

ABCs

Thursday evenings would always creep in
and we knew that meant one thing:
    Ka Kha Ga Gha.

While Mummy buttoned us into smart clothes —
    Ka Kha Ga
              Gha —
shovelled *rotli* and *ringra nu shak* into our mouths —
    Ka Kha
        Ga
        Gha —
piled us into our red Cavalier —
    Ka Kha Ga?
          Gha —
chimed the way —
    Ka Ka
        Kha Kha
            Ga —
through the — *Ka*
    steel gates — *Kha*
        heaved — *Ga*
           us out — *Gha*
              and we dragged — *Ka*
                our legs — *Kha*
                  all the way to our door —

Ka Kha Ga — slipped
    Ga Gha — in
        as Sir settled — *Ka*
        the din — *Kha*
            and began — *Ga*
            to take note:
                — *Shruti?*
                  — *Gha.*
                    — *Pardon?*
                      — *Er... present!*
                      I mean, present!

Again

My phone vibrates. I brace myself,
and once again his messages pile in.

Shruti, I feel needy, why doesn't she need me?
I stay up till five, help her with assignments,
so why is she at dinner with some other guy then?
I'm just pathetic, a doormat, I'm nothing – hey,
where are you? Hey, are you listening?

I'm here, I sigh.
He carries on.

She decides when we hang out, hold hands or hug,
yet I need permission to touch her, to miss her?
And when I ask her why, she shushes me like a child,
says it's paranoia. Shruti, are you there? Answer me,
please, you're my only friend.

I'm sat playing Tetris but tell him I'm busy.

Hey, Shruti, I hacked her email, couldn't help it,
needed to know who she talks to in private.
Shit – now I'm anxious, shit – now I'm scared.
Quick, Shruti, what do I do? Hey, tell me, do I tell her
the truth?

I wonder, should I even answer?
He's asked me about her again and again.
So many times I've told him, she's selfish, a user,
don't lose self-respect trying to please her –
leave her. But my words are nothing but dust
in the face of the patterns he refuses to purge.

Two years, since uni, he's sent me updates
from Delhi, updates that strain me,
updates that drain me.

3am he shakes me awake, tells me he's stoned,
6am he's drunk, at 9 he's waiting for the counsellor,
lunchtime he's crying, 4pm he wants Prozac,
5pm he's worn me down, at 7 he writes her a ten-page
apology and at 10, he's self-harming, scoring his
skin with her name, but by then I've slipped into sleep.

I used to wake at dawn, it all flooding back.
I'd scramble for my phone, dread the hundred
unread messages, but I know now not to worry
because he'll be there in the morning.

Shruti, the doc changed my meds!
    I ignore him, because he'll be there in the morning.
Shruti, they don't know what's wrong!
    I ignore him, because he'll be there in the morning.
Shruti, she won't take my calls!
    I ignore him, because he'll be there in the morning.
Shruti, I need you, she's gone!
    I ignore him, because he'll be there in the morning.

It's morning and my phone is not vibrating.

Sameer,

hey,

are you there?

Hushed

This is not the first time your
eyes won't meet me   I know

you would rather trail an ant
on its drunken stroll   join

dots on your speckled floor or
concertina your sari edge

but the silence between
us will shrivel some

time   and when it does you will
have to tell why your head

droops like a willow limb   why
the tears bunch your

lashes like bunting rows
why you tremor in the

lightless hours   a web in
winter wind   you will leave

me no choice but to pray he
fists   swings

mulches you to blood   makes
abstract your face   pray

his cruel is no more
hushed

62p

Beaumont Leys Library.

It's two o'clock, or three.
Gilded shafts of light streak across
the blush-carpet floor. The place is hushed,
the post-school rush still a while away.
An old couple lingers in the Large Print aisle
and a father feeds a story to the toddler
on his knees.

I'm at the front desk, stapling paper,
when I hear that well-known, slow
squeak of rubber soles.

Hi, Cathy.
Cathy's thirty-eight, a Miss,
comes in Tuesdays, mostly unnoticed,
the same bobbled mustard jumper,
and mousy neck-length hair wedged
behind her ears. Her hazel eyes are
always speechless. She doesn't say much,
but when she does, she can't believe
the words are hers.

She hands me the Frozen DVD for sale.
That's £1, please. Cathy dumps a
plastic bag of pennies on the counter,
fishes one out and slides it to the side.

One, she breathes, lines etched across
her brow, *two… three… four —*
Cathy, can I help?

No, I'll do it myself.
Five… six… seven… eight…

By now a fretful queue is taking shape.
Mothers clutching picture books,
glaring at watches, then at Cathy.
Fifteen… sixteen… Parents shaking heads,
babies threatening to cry.

I apologise, steer them to another computer,
scan, stamp books as quick as I can.
In between I glance at Cathy.
Twenty-nine… thirty… When I'm done,
I hurry to her. The counting has stopped.
How much have you got?
38p.

She looks at me, not quite comprehending.
That's not enough, Cathy. She stares hard at
the pennies she's laid down like honeycomb.
How much do I need?
62p. And she starts again from scratch.

One… two… A line forms once more,
I need to tell her to stop –
Nine… ten —
You don't have enough, Cathy, but she
won't hear me. Then suddenly –

Excuse me? A ponytailed brunette calls me over.
How much does she need?
62p. She slips it into my palm, beams,
and is gone. I make my way back to Cathy,
scoop up her coins and tell her, *You can have
the DVD; a lady's just given you 62p.*

Cathy gapes, can't speak,
but her ever-silent eyes glisten,
tell a thousand things of
kindness.

Summertime

Tell me again about yesterday.
Tell me about the times we flew after butterflies
knowing they'd take us someplace secret.
Tell me about tipping sand out of open-toe sandals,
about watermelon dribbling down our chins and
our mothers flailing after us with paper napkins.
Tell me about sitting cross-legged on grass
looping daisies into crowns.
Tell me about ice cubes cracking in Ribena,
about bubbles wafting by,
about warm breezes scattering our unruly hair.
Tell me about our restlessness,
about lollies bluing our tongues.
Tell me about never seeing night,
about crisping peppers on bamboo skewers.
Tell me about shooting water at the boys across the street,
about water-bombs wobbling back
through the air and crashing at our feet.
Tell me about racing first thing out from our homes,
about skipping ropes slapping the roads.
Tell me about stacked jam sandwiches and picnics in the park.
Tell me about paddling pools filling with flies,
about storms fracturing the sky,
about the smell of earth after the rain.
Tell me about cupping wishes in our palms
before sending them to heaven.
But more than anything,
tell me about the sun,
about its unabashed blaze,
about our squints as we tried – foolish – to
push through its glare.
Tell me about it soaking us in gold,
about it warming our bones,
about the amber glow when our eyes were closed.
Tell me about the shimmer on our limbs,
about the markings on our skin where our clothes had been;
tell me again and again about the sun, as I've forgotten.

These days I shrink from its rays,
cling to the shade or stay in.
        I'd rather drive down pills of vitamin D
  than be caught in a patch of light,
        because I've learnt, our mothers want for their sons,
            girls who've stayed out of the sun,
                who'll give birth to children unsunned.
        Men, too, dream of fair and lovely,
    dismiss the rest as dark and ugly;
                and our screens cast out the sun-kissed,
                    flash faces instead that are dipped in creams.
        Here's a world I can't escape,
    a world carving complexes out of complexions.
Tell me again about yesterday.
        Tell me about the times we didn't care,
                didn't see skin as dark or fair.
        Tell me again.

                Tell me again.

Notes

Desh – Country
Om shantih shantih shantih – A Sanskrit mantra invoking peace
Vidai – The Hindu wedding ritual of the bride bidding farewell to her family
Rotla – Millet flatbread
Dikro – A Gujarati term of endearment
Kaki – Father's younger brother's wife
Masi – Mother's sister
Fui – Father's sister
Mami – Mother's brother's wife
Masa – Mother's sister's husband
Fua – Father's sister's husband
Kaka – Father's younger brother
Ada – Father's elder brother
Sa Re Ga Ma Pa – The first five solfa syllables in the Indian classical music system
Raga Shivranjani – A sequence of notes in Indian classical music evoking a melancholy mood
Rotli – Chapatti
Ringra nu shak – Aubergine curry

Acknowledgements

Thanks to the editors of the following publications, where some of these poems first appeared, sometimes in earlier versions: *Best Poetry Book in the World* (Burning Eye Books, 2017) and *Second Place Rosette: Poems about Britain* (The Emma Press, 2018).

I am eternally grateful to Mark Goodwin, Kerry Featherstone, Maria Taylor and Tom Sastry for their guidance, critical comments and encouragement in the making of this pamphlet, and to all the creatives who have inspired and helped me along the way.

Thanks to Burning Eye, Clive Birnie, Bridget Hart, Harriet Evans and Liv Torc for your patience, and for bringing *That Which Can Be Heard* to life.

Thank you to the wonderfully talented Priya Barot and Comal Patel for the cover art and design, respectively.

As always, love and gratitude to my parents and my sister, and to the family and friends who have supported me unconditionally; I couldn't have done this without you.

About the Author

Shruti Chauhan is a British Indian poet and performer based in Leicester. She has performed both nationally and internationally, and in 2015, she toured *Three the Hard Way – Part 2* with Jean 'Binta' Breeze MBE and Lydia Towsey. Shruti was voted Best Spoken Word Performer at the 2018 Saboteur Awards and won the National Poetry Library's Instapoetry competition the same year. Shruti wrote the song lyrics for the BBC Four documentary, *My Asian Family – The Musical* (2018) as part of the BBC's Big British Asian Summer season. *That Which Can Be Heard* is her first pamphlet.

9 781911 570493